GOD'S ADVICE
to the
NATIONS
of the
WORLD

*How to Overcome Depression; How to
Be a Good Parent; How to Deal with Pollution*

REV. MICHAEL WALKER

God's Advice to the Nations of the World by Rev. Michael Walker

ISBN 978-1-952027-72-7 (Paperback)
ISBN 978-1-952027-73-4 (Hardback)

This book is written to provide information and motivation to readers. Its purpose is not to render any type of psychological, legal, or professional advice of any kind. The content is the sole opinion and expression of the author, and not necessarily that of the publisher.

Copyright © 2020 by Rev. Michael Walker

All rights reserved. No part of this book may be reproduced, transmitted, or distributed in any form by any means, including, but not limited to, recording, photocopying, or taking screenshots of parts of the book, without prior written permission from the author or the publisher. Brief quotations for noncommercial purposes, such as book reviews, permitted by Fair Use of the U.S. Copyright Law, are allowed without written permissions, as long as such quotations do not cause damage to the book's commercial value. For permissions, write to the publisher, whose address is stated below.

Printed in the United States of America.

New Leaf Media, LLC
175 S. 3rd Street, Suite 200
Columbus, OH 43215
www.thenewleafmedia.com

All rights reserved. No part of this publication may be reproduced, stored in a retrieval system, or transmitted in any form by any means, electronic, mechanical, photocopying, recording, or otherwise without the prior written permission of both the copyright owner and the publisher of this book.

Disclaimer. This is to certify that whilst every precaution is undertaken for originality neither the author nor publisher has any liability to any person or entity with respect to any: similarities, errors, oversight or inaccuracies contain therein.

CONTENTS

PART 1

How To Overcome Depression

Introduction ... 1
Chapter 1 What Can Cause Depression? ... 3
Chapter 2 How to overcome the spirits of Depression, you don't have to commit suicide ... 7
Chapter 3 Singing And Giving Thanks To God ... 15
Chapter 4 Having Abundant Life ... 21
Chapter 5 The thoughts of a young mother suffering from depression ... 27
Conclusion ... 29

PART 2

How to Be a Good Parent

Introduction ... 33
Chapter 1 What Is the Duty of Parents to Their Children? ... 35
Chapter 2 The Duty of Fathers ... 39
Chapter 3 The Duty of a Mother ... 47
Chapter 4 The Duty of Grandparents ... 53

Chapter 5	Advice to Women	55
Chapter 6	Advice to Fathers	57
Chapter 7	Prisons should be Places of Training	59
Chapter 8	Drug Abuse	63
Conclusion		67

PART 3

How to deal with Pollution

Introduction		73
Chapter 1	How to Fix Our Polluted Environment	77
Chapter 2	The Increase of the Motor Vehicle	83
Chapter 3	Cyclists on the Road	85
Chapter 4	The Pressure on the NHS and Our Hospitals	87
Chapter 5	Terrorism on the Roads	89
Conclusion		93

About the Author	95
About the Book	97

PART 1

How To Overcome Depression

INTRODUCTION

What is depression? It is a sickness, which any one can have at any time in their life. When someone is going through depression, he or she will feel so down, that they will not even want to live any longer, they can feel that life is not worth living any more, and daily they are in that state, sometimes for months, and even years.

They have tried medication, and nothing works, and sometimes the medication causes them to get worse.

Some of the symptoms can cause them to be like a recluse. They don't want to see anybody, not opening their mails, not answering calls, refusing to work, just wanting to sleep every day, refusing to get out of bed, feeling completely empty and drained of energy.

I hope that this book will open the eyes of our people, so that they will know what to do when depression strikes and those devils desire to kill them. That they may also know what is going on in their lives.

Here is some ammunition from the Word of God, which will help you. When you are attacked by demons, you may draw from the written Word of God, which is the sword of the Spirit.

Only the Word of God can destroy those devils.

In (Ephesians 6:17, 18, KJV) the Bible says that we should take the sword of the Spirit, which is the Word of God, and we should pray with all types of prayer:

Intercessory, Travailing, Prevailing etc.

Prayer is talking to the Father, asking him for his help in your daily life. It is vital that you believe and talk to the One above, he will always hear what you are saying, and he will never tell you to, 'shut up, you talk too much.' He is the greatest listener, and he will never be tired of hearing you talking to him daily.

He is waiting to hear from you in your hour of need, why not give him a call, he is always on the line, there is no voice mail, it is a direct line for all to call, and receive help, any time we are in trouble.

In the Bible, also called The Book of life, Jesus says, 'the words which I speak to you they are spirit, and they are life.' Therefore please make the greatest investment of your life by buying a Bible, and studying it, and applying his Word to whatever needs that you have.

The Devil does not want you to know how to defeat him when he attacks you, with depression, anxiety and panic attacks.

In (St. John 10:10KJV) Jesus says,

'The thief (Devil) cometh not but for to steal, and to kill and to destroy: I am come that they might have life, and that they might have it more abundantly.

This means he Jesus, comes to make us anew so that we can live forever.

CHAPTER 1

What Can Cause Depression?

Let's ask ourselves this question, 'What are some of the things which can cause depression?' The truth is that it can start with many things, including problems: living with others, regrets about something you may have done or haven't done, loved ones turning against you, work problems, financial problems, and even rejection.

Imagine if one of your loved ones turned against you. Your spouse—the person of your dreams, the one you wish to live with for the rest of your life—tells you one day, 'I want you out of my life. I don't love you anymore.'

You have tried and tried to reconcile with the person, but it is like you are up against a brick wall. The person says, 'I have moved on with my life, so you must move on with yours.'

The next thing you see is a file for divorce proceeding. You are in the courts for no reason you can think of. Your life is shattered. At that time, you wonder, *what am I living for?* You have lost all you held so dear; it can be devastating. Satan sees you are so vulnerable and weak. Then all his demons flock to you and tells you, 'life is not worth living, and you should take your life.'

The devils speak to you, and you hear many voices. Satan loves to talk, but never talk to him or do what he tells you to do. At that time, prayer is vital.

You may say, 'I don't know how to pray,' but just ask God to help you. I assure you he is listening to your faintest cry, and he wants to help you.

Never do what Satan's voices tell you to do. It is the devil that is oppressing and depressing you, trying to make you lose the everlasting life and joy Jesus Christ provided for you.

If you take your life, it will be worse than what you are presently going through. You will find yourself in hell, a place of torment and home to Satan and his devils. You will be in torment with the fire which shall never be quenched and where no water is. Then Satan will laugh at you because he has deceived and overcome you.

But when depression comes, in whatever way it comes, it is devastating. If the person does not get help, suicide can result.

Too many young people commit suicide because they don't know not what to do when faced with Satan and his hosts.

Some youths may turn to drugs and alcohol. But your best option is to turn to God. He can help you in your time of trouble and hour of need. He says, 'When my father and my mother forsake me, then the Lord will take me up,' (Psalm 27:10).

Jesus also stated that, he will never forsake us, and he will never leave us. His word is his bond; he cannot go back on his word.

He said in (St. Matthew 24:35, KJV) 'heaven and earth shall pass away but my words shall not pass away.'

God will never abandon you. You are the most precious thing he has created, and as the Father, he will always be there for you, in whatever situation you are in.

He is waiting to hear from you. We are here to teach the nations about our Father, the one who will never desert us and will come to us when we call.

In the olden days, there were no medications as we have today. So the people who believed, called on God, and he delivered them. He is just the same in every generation. He can deliver you if you faithfully call on him today.

CHAPTER 2

*How to overcome the spirits of Depression,
you don't have to commit suicide*

First, we need to acknowledge that we are depressed. If we are in denial, no one can help us. But when we face our depression and ask for help, we can be helped.

The best way to overcome depression is to go to God's Word for help. For many people experiencing depression, the last person they want to hear about is God. But he is the first one they should turn to because he has the right answer to help them.

Let us look at Jesus's earthly ministry. We read in (St Mark 5KJV) that he met a man plagued by a legion of devils, who were living in him. He used to sleep in the: mountains, graveyards, and even tombs. They chained him, but he broke the chains. They even tied him with ropes, but he would break through them. He was like a wild man. Nights and days, the Bible says, he cried and cut himself but no one could help him.

Then one day he met Jesus. He ran and fell at his feet, and worshipped him. Jesus rebuked the devils and told them to come out of the man. Then the devils begged Jesus to allow them to go into some swine which were feeding on a mountain, and Jesus allowed them. Immediately they left the man, and he was cured and was restored to his right mind. There was no more mental sickness.

The story continues, that the swine which the devils went into ran violently down the hill and into the sea, killing themselves. They were overpowered but would not allow the devils to live in them. They would rather die than to let the demons control them.

We cannot see the devils, since they are spirit beings but they can see us. They can come into us, live in us, and cause us to do all the evil works Satan wants to do.

We know that God created man and woman to live in us but because he is a Spirit, he cannot be seen. Therefore he initially created us for his habitation. However, because he created us with self-will; he has also given us the option of choice, to be like him. He put man and woman in the Garden of Eden and allowed them to choose. Both made the wrong choice and allowed the devil to control them. God knew we would all make wrong choices, so he made a way to help us make the right choices by sending Jesus Christ. He helps us make the right decisions when we have him—not the devil—living in our hearts.

It is your choice of whom you allow to live in your heart, God or the devil. Make your choice a good one as it is your last chance to choose in this life.

Who causes us to suffer from depression?

The devils who oppress us. The greatest help we can get, is from the Word of God.

Satan's greatest weapons against us are **Discouragement** and **Depression**. When he uses these particular depravities, only God can deliver us.

Believe it or not, the Bible recounts that even our beloved Jesus underwent a bout of depression. We read the account of the night when he was betrayed. He went into the garden of Gethsemane.

In (St Matthew 26: KJV) he told his disciples that his soul was exceedingly sorrowful even unto death. He asked them to pray with him. He went a bit further, the Bible says, and fell to the ground and prayed, asking his Father if it was possible, he should make another way to escape the terror of sin.

And when he had finished praying, he returned to his disciples. Finding them sleeping, he asked them, 'What, could you not watch with me one hour?' Then he went away and prayed again. When he returned, he found them sleeping again.

The third time he went away and then came back again, they were still sleeping. He told them that their spirit was willing, but their flesh was weak.

Let us read the account of St. Paul to the Jews about how Jesus suffered the night he was arrested.

(Hebrews 5:7, 8, KJV) tells us that in the days of his flesh, when he had offered up prayers and supplication, with strong crying and tears to him who was able to save him from death, he was heard. Though he was a son, he learned obedience through the things he suffered.

If the Creator of the world as a human, could feel depression, we should learn how he overcame it and follow his words.

As we can see in the scriptures, Jesus used prayer to overcome his depression, and we can use the same method to help us to also overcome our depressions.

In Psalm 42, King David declares his soul was cast down, but he would hope in, and pray to God. Let us see what he did when he was depressed and take some of his advice when we are going through depression. This is the greatest Psalm and can help us if we follow its guidance. The psalm begins to show us how we should seek God like a deer seek water when they are thirsty.

Rev. Michael Walker

(Psalm 42:1–11KJV) reads:

1 'As the hart panteth after the water brook so panteth my soul after thee, Oh God.

2 My soul thirst for God, for the living God: when shall I come and appear before God?

3 My tears have been my meat day, and night, while they continually say unto me where is thy God?

4 When I remember these things, I pour out my soul in me: for I had gone with the multitude, I went with them to the house of God, with the voice of joy and praise, with the multitude that kept holyday.

5 Why are you cast down, Oh my soul? and why are you disquieted in me? hope thou in God: for I shall yet praise him for the help of his countenance.

6 Oh my God, my soul is cast down within me: therefore will I remember thee from the land of Jordan, and of the Hermonites, from the hill Mizar.

7 Deep calleth unto deep at the noise of thy waterspouts: all thy waves and thy billows are gone over me.

8 Yet the Lord will command his loving kindness in the day time, and in the night his song shall be with me, and my prayer unto the God of my life.

9 I will say unto God my rock, why hast thou forgotten me? why go I mourning because of the oppression of the enemy?

10 As with a sword in my bones, mine enemies reproach me; while they say daily unto me, Where is thy God?

11 Why are thou cast down, Oh my soul? and why are thou disquieted within me? hope thou in God: for I shall yet praise him, who is the health of my countenance, and my God'.

Having read through Psalm 42 and seen how the man, whom God says that he has found David, a man after his own heart, let us look at how David was troubled by the enemy.

From the time that God had chosen David as a King, over Israel, he went through all kinds of troubles. Beginning from the time he slew the Giant Goliath, his life was threatened by the then, Kind Saul whom God had rejected from being King. David escaped many times, from the pursuit of Saul, and his men. He had to live like a fugitive, because he was chosen by God, to be the King of Israel, when Saul died.

We have seen in the Bible, during his reign as king that even his son Absalom had a coup against him, and he had to run from the Palace, because his own son wanted to kill him.

I put it to you and know you will agree with me that the man had a reason to be depressed.

His house was in turmoil, one of his Sons, Rape one of the sister, and the brother of the sister killed that same brother because of the rape of his sister, what you would say if that happen to you, and your house, and there is nothing that you can do, how you would feel in such a time as that.

One thing that we can see, that God did not reject King David, nor forsake him, in all his times of troubles God was with him, and he protected him.

The Psalms are a wonderful means of comfort for us, when those spirits of depression attack us, we need to read them regularly, and meditate upon them daily.

Let us look at the words in,

(Psalm 6:1-10, KJV)

1 'O Lord, rebuke me not in thy anger, neither chasten me in thy hot displeasure.

2 Have mercy upon me, O Lord; for I am weak: O Lord, heal me; for my bones are vexed.

3 My soul is also sore vexed: but thou, O Lord, how long.?

4 Return, O Lord, deliver my soul: O save me for thy mercy's sake.

5 For in death there is no remembrance of thee: in the grave who shall give thee thanks?

6 I am weary with my groaning; all the night make I my bed to swim,; I water my couch with my tears.

7 My eyes is consumed because of grief; it waxeth old because of all mine enemies.

8 Depart from me, all you workers of iniquities; for the Lord hath heard the voice of my weeping.

9 The Lord hath heard my supplication: the Lord will receive my prayer.

10 Let all my enemies be ashamed and sore vexed: let them return and be ashamed suddenly.'

When you are facing a barrage of trouble, it is good to know that God is right by your side. He will not forsake you nor forget you, and this is the time that you need to draw closer to him.

Some people when they are going through any type of trouble, they turn away from God, but we can see that when David was having these troubles he called on God to deliver him and God answered him and delivered him. I assure you that he can do the same for you and more.

Here is another way in which we can overcome depression, it is to think positively.

Our thoughts are a vital weapon which the Devil can use against us.

Each minute of the day we are thinking on something, if we have negative thoughts then that can help to depress us.

Our mind is the battlefield where the war for our soul is fought.

When we win the war for our mind then we can overcome the Devil.

He will bring evil thoughts to our mind, but how can we overcome those thoughts.

We must always rebuke the devils who will bombard us with these evil thoughts.

Never ever let these evil thoughts rest in your heart, reject them and do what Jesus did when he was tempted. He told the Devil to get thee hence, which means go away from me. We can use these words for as long as we live. It will always be a potent weapon against the Devil, but when we use it, we must always ask Jesus to wash us in his blood and cleanse us from all evil thoughts.

The blood which he shed on the cross for us, is always flowing, to save and to cleanse everyone who comes to him for help, no one is turned away.

The Bible also tells us what we should think on.

Let us read the advice from Brother Paul to the people of Philippi.

(Philippians 4: 4-9, KJV)

'Rejoice in the Lord always: and again I say, Rejoice.

5. Let your moderation be known unto all men. The Lord is at hand.

6. Be careful for nothing; but in every thing by prayer and supplication with thanksgiving let your request be made known unto God.

7. And the peace of God, which passeth all understanding, shall keep your hearts and minds through Christ Jesus.

8. Finally, brethren, whatsoever things are true, whatsoever things are honest, whatsoever things are just, whatsoever things pure, whatsoever things are lovely, whatsoever things are of good report; if there be any virtue, if there be any praise think on these things.

9. Those things, which ye have both learned, and received, and heard and see in me, do: and the God of peace shall be with you'.

If we read the Words of God and apply them to our hearts daily, we would receive great benefits from it.

The Bible took over fifteen hundred years to compile, and it can deal with all our short comings; it is for all peoples and all generations.

But sad to say that our generation has rejected it to our own down fall. It should be taught in the schools, and in the homes, so that our children will know where to find help when they are facing the attacks by demons,

or when they are in any trouble. You don't have to commit suicide it is the wrong way out of your situation. Remember prayer is the right way out of that evil situation in which you have found yourself.

CHAPTER 3

Singing And Giving Thanks To God

When we look at the Scriptures, which the Apostle Paul wrote to the people of Ephesus, about the way that they should follow Christ, he told them that they should not be drunk, with wine, wherein is excess, but they should be filled with the Spirit. He encouraged them to speak to themselves, in Psalms, and hymns, and spiritual songs. He also prompted them to sing and make melody in their hearts, to the Lord.

(Eph.5: 17- 19.KJV)
17 'Wherefore be ye not unwise, but understanding what the will of the Lord is.
18 And be not drunk with wine, wherein is excess; but be filled with the Spirit;
19 Speaking to yourself in Psalm and hymns and spiritual songs, singing and making melody in your heart to the Lord.'

Singing spiritual songs, is one of the greatest ways of pulling yourself out of depression. It gives joy to the soul, meaning to both body, and spirit.

Music on a whole will help to drive away the Devils which come to harass and depress you, they hate Gospel Music especially.

The Bible tells us a story of the first King of Israel named Saul. He was chosen when the people of Israel rejected the direct rule of God, and asked for a King like the other nations. God accepted their request, but the first assignment which God gave their King Saul he disobeyed, and did not carry out the assignment, as God had instructed him. Therefore, God rejected him from being king, over his people.

He was then fully taken over by an evil spirit which possessed him.

<u>Music</u> was the only thing which brought him solace and which caused the evil spirit to leave him. His servants encouraged him to find an expert musician. They recommended David son of Jesse, who could skilfully play the harp. Each time David played, the King would have great peace, because the tormenting devils would depart.

(1st Sam. 16:14-17KJV)

14. 'But the Spirit of the Lord departed from Saul, and an evil Spirit from the Lord troubled him.

15. And Saul's servant said unto him, behold now, an evil Spirit from God trouble thee.

16. Let our lord now command thy servants which are before thee, to seek out a man, who is a cunning player on a harp: and it shall come to pass, when the evil spirit from God is upon thee, that he shall play with his hand, and thou shall be well.

17 And Saul said unto his servants, provide me now a man that can play well, and bring him to me.'

The Devil wants to break your spirit, and get your body so weak, that you cannot resist him. Jesus told his disciples on the night when he was in the Garden of Gethsemane, 'my soul is exceedingly sorrowful, even unto death.' That to me would mean that in his humanity, he was depressed.

He told them that they should watch and pray so that they would not enter into temptation. What is temptation? We may query. It is when the Devil is telling you to do evil things, to do terrible things that are not right.

That is how he had deceived Eve in the Garden of Eden, and plunged the World into all the troubles which we are facing on Earth today.

So we can see that the Devil is attacking the spirit so that he can destroy the body and soul. But if we would pray to God, then we would be able to defeat him.

You may say to me, 'but I can't pray or I am too worried, and I can't find the words to say.' Now prayer is not only when we pray for a long time and speak a lot of words, prayer can be just two words as, 'Help Lord!' Even when we cry to him he understands why.

Let us look at when we were born, we did not know how to talk, and when we needed something what did we do? We cried and our parents came to us. They as earthly parents gave us what we needed. Therefore we should likewise cry to the Lord our heavenly Father and he will understand, and come to our rescue.

You may say that you do not believe in the Lord. However, this would be a good time for you to say, 'if there is a God, please help me,' and don't stop saying that until he responds to your request, don't give up; you will need to exercise faith, and believe that you will get an answer.

He can respond in many ways, he can send someone to help you, he can let his peace overshadow you, he can give you a dream, he can send someone to pray for you, and to encourage you.

Rev. Michael Walker

This is a true story that has happened to a young lady, who was in a very deep depression. She had four children, the youngest was about three months. She had no one to help her, no father to help them. She had to take her three eldest children, about seven miles to school, and pick them up again in the evening. Twice she tried to commit suicide.

One day she had to go and bring home her children, but she was so depressed, she could not drive. She asked God to help her to go for her children, and she decided to take the bus. Her intention was to come off the bus, and take the train, to continue the rest of her journey.

When she reached near to the train station, she heard a voice say to her, 'stay on the bus, to the end of the bus destination.' She obeyed the voice.

Then strangely enough someone behind her began to play with her baby of about three months old. He asked her if the child was Christened, she told him no, and that she also had three more children to be Christened. He then told her that he was a Minister of Religion. He also told her that he could christen them.

She then begin to tell him of the problems that she was having. She told him that all that she could see in her life was only darkness. The minister then prayed for her, and assured her, 'you will see no more darkness,' she reported that the total darkness had immediately vanished. She testified that she felt like she had an out of body experience. She was then very happy, and was feeling better, and went for her children and brought them home.

She then began to tell her friends, what had happened to her while on the bus. Now the lord is on her side helping her, and her children. The evil one has tried many more times to bring darkness on her, but now God has given her a Minister whom she can call on for help.

God works in many mysterious ways, and he wants to help us if we would allow him. All we need is to ask him, and believe that he hears, and he is willing to help us if we only believe.

The Devil who bring depression on us, does it for one purpose, and that is to kill us. That is why you will hear voices in your head, telling you to kill yourself. Do not obey those evil voices. If you kill yourself it will be worse, because your spirit will go to a place which is worse than here. It's a place of torment where you will be suffering forever, and cannot die. The Bible called that place Hell, where the Devil is.

You need to decide where you will live in the next life, with Jesus or with the Devil. Man, and woman, is not just body, we have a spirit, who is living inside of us, which will live forever. We are here to decide where we want to live after this life is over.

Let's face it, we are not here forever, we must go, so don't let the Devil tell you that you are not worth anything, and when you die there is nothing you are finished.

We are the most precious thing that God has created. You need to believe that your life is worth living.

Believe what God says about you, not what the evil one says, he is a liar, and a deceiver, and he means you no good. All he wants to do is to destroy, and to kill you, but God loves you, and wants to bless you, and give you a long life.

Remember, Jesus says in St. John 10:10 'the thief comes, not but for to steal, and to kill, and to destroy, but I am come that they might have life, and have it more abundantly.' That simply means for you to live forever with him.

CHAPTER 4

Having Abundant Life

When does that abundant life begin with Jesus Christ? It starts right here on Earth, when we invite him into our heart he will come in, and our eternal life begins at that very moment.

We need to understand that God is a Spirit, and although we cannot see him, he can see us. And just as we breathe the air around us, and it lives in us, and gives us life, he can live in us, and give us everlasting life.

The Scriptures says in,

(St John 1:12, KJV)
'But as many as receive him, to them gave he power to become the sons, of God, even to them that believe on his name:'

When we accept Jesus as our Lord, and Saviour, we become born again; we are now a new creature. The Bible says, old things are pass away, and behold all things are become new.

We now can see spiritual things, which before we could not see. Our spiritual eyes is now open to the invisible things which are all around us, and now we can understand what life is all about. We now walk by faith not by sight.

It is vital that we look into the Word of God for guidance.

(Psalm 119:105KJV) says,

'Thy word is a lamp unto my feet, and a light unto my path'.

That means we can be guided by his words daily, if we make a habit of reading it regularly, and let it be a part of us.

His word can renew our minds, and transform us from the old ways of thinking.

The Devil wants to control your mind, to make you mentally disturb, and then destroy you. You need to begin to fight to keep your mind, from being controlled by the Devil.

The Bible says in,

(1st Timothy 6:12KJV)

'Fight the good fight of faith, and lay hold on eternal life, whereunto thou art also called, and hast professed a good profession before many witnesses.'

This is what the Devil is trying to take from you, your faith in God. He doesn't want you to live forever, but Jesus says that I am come to give life everlasting.

You should be willing to fight for life, so that you can live forever with Jesus.

I am not saying that when you have Jesus living inside of you, you will not be depressed, your world may crumble but he will see you through your time of difficulties.

Believe me, I know what I am talking about, even the greatest men, and women of God go through times of depression, but he will bring us through it, so that we can have the experience to help others when they are attacked by the Devil.

Let us look at a story in the Bible about a man named Job.

Job Chap 1: Told us that he was a wealthy man, at that time the richest man in the East. (Job 1: 6-12, KJV) 'Now there was a day when the sons of God came to present themselves before the Lord, and Satan came also among them.

7 And the Lord said unto Satan, whence comets thou? Then Satan answered the Lord, and said, 'From going through and fro in the Earth, and from walking up and down in it.'

8 And the Lord said unto Satan, 'hast thou considered my servant Job, that there is none like him in the Earth, a perfect and an upright man, one that feared God, and escheweth evil?'

9 Then Satan answered the Lord, and said, 'doth Job fear God for nought?

10 Hast not thou made a hedge about him, and about his house, and about all that he hath on every side? thou hast blessed the work of his hand , and his substance is increased in the Land.

11 But put forth your hands now, and touch all that he hath, and he will curse thee to thy face.'

12 And the Lord said unto Satan, 'Behold, all that he hath is in thy power; only upon himself put not forth thy hand.'

So Satan went forth from the presence of the Lord.' And he began to destroy Jobs wealth, all his cattle was stolen. Then his ten children were killed by a storm which blew down the house where they were having a birthday party, and all were killed.

When Job heard these bad news, one after the other, he did not curse God, as the Devil thought that he would, he begin to worship, and to give thanks to God, his words were, 'the Lord giveth, and the Lord taketh away, blessed be the name of the Lord.'

However the Devil was still determined to destroy him.

Rev. Michael Walker

(Job 2: 1-6KJV)

'Again there was a day when the sons of God came to present themselves before the Lord, and Satan came also among them to present himself before the Lord.

2 And the Lord said unto Satan, from whence comest thou? And Satan answered the Lord, and said, from going to and fro, in the earth, and from walking up and down in it.

3 And the Lord said unto Satan, Hast thou considered my servant Job, that there is none like him in the earth, a perfect and an upright man, one that feareth God, and escheweth evil? and still he holdeth fast his integrity, although thou movedst me against him, to destroy him, to destroy him without cause.'

4 And Satan answered the Lord, and said, Skin for skin, yea, all that a man hath will he give for his life.

5 But put forth your hand now, and touch his bone and his flesh, and he will curse thee to thy face.

6 And the Lord said unto Satan, Behold, he is in your hand; but save his life.

The story says that the Devil went from the presence of the Lord, and smote Job with boils from the crown of his head to the sole of his feet, and Job sat in ashes, and scraped himself with a potsherd, and he smelled horrible.

Then one day his wife, the only one whom he had left of his family, asked him this horrible question, 'do you still hold your integrity, why don't you curse God and die?' However, Job was a wise man, who said to his wife, 'you speak as one of the foolish woman, shall we receive well at the Lord's hand, and should we curse him because evil comes upon us?'

The story says that in all these trials, which Job went through he did not charge God wrongfully.

When Jesus was here he commented on the patience of Job, and kindness of God to him after he had endured, those trials, that God had made him twice as rich, and he gave him ten more children, seven sons, and three more daughters, the same number of which the Devil had killed. The girls was so beautiful that Job gave them equal share of the inheritance with the sons.

Today it is the same Devil that we face. The only difference is that we have gone so far astray from God, that we no longer understand what the Devil is doing.

Remember what Jesus says in the scriptures in St. John 10:10 'The thief cometh not, but for to steal, and to kill, and to destroy: I am come that they might have life, and that they might have it more abundantly.' This means that you and I can have the life which he brings to us.

When the devils are talking to you, and telling you to kill yourself. Don't ever do what he is telling you; command him to leave you. These are the words which Jesus told him, 'get thee hence Satan,' means get away from me, you can say that a million times, and ask Jesus Christ for his help.

CHAPTER 5

The thoughts of a young mother suffering from depression

Here is the thoughts of a young mother, struggling to look after her four children alone, with only her Mother giving a helping hand, some of the time. She had been through dark days, and tried twice to commit suicide, until she met a man of God who prayed for her, and the darkness flew, and he continue to give Godly support to her and her children.

"Living with depression and anxiety, always feeling lost in my own feelings, what shall tomorrow brings, will I sing songs of sorrow, what shall tomorrow brings, as my brain ticks over wishing my life would be over?

What shall tomorrow brings, will I be happy, will I be sad, shall I do good, shall I do bad.

I watch the World go by, not knowing how I feel, all I know this pain is real.

My soul feels numb, fighting the Demons in my head, countless tears I shed, bursting with frustration, and can't deal with miscommunication.

I lay there at nights, it is the worst time to try and see the sight of what could, or might have been, all I see is darkness, no light, when will things be better for me.

Why is it when one door closes, another never opens, why is it when I climb up the ladder, my life crumbles and shatters

What shall tomorrow brings, will I be singing that life is worth living, I watch the World goes by pretending that I am fine, and everything is divine, if I think that I'm alright then I might just see the light, I pray for my future to be bright, I say Lord show me the light.

I wait for the day when I can say I'm doing good, with my mother standing there beside me, saying I know you could make it."

It is so sad to know that this is the story of many young mothers across the World today, struggling to keep their children, and looking after them in our society, which are so fractured. Many of the Fathers have abandoned their responsibility to care for their children.

Let me commend all the Mothers who are struggling to bring up their children alone, you are doing a wonderful job.

But let me say to those fathers who have abandoned their children, one day the Heavenly Father will call you to give account for those children which you are going around and having, without taking responsibility for them. You will have to give account one day to him.

There is an old saying, it goes like this, 'children are not Iron pots.'

That means they will grow, they are human beings they need to be taken care of, and to be valued as a gift from God.

There is another saying, 'children are our heritage.'

They are the ones who will grow up, and work to pay our pensions, and look after us when we get old and feeble.

So brothers, let me encourage you, to change your ways, and take care of your offspring.

They are a gift from the Father above.

Let's get back to the old ways of caring, and looking after one another, which is what the good book (Bible)says, and when we begin to do this then we would find a better world to live in.

CONCLUSION

Now that we have come to the end of this book, I hope that it will be a good help to all those who read it, and that they will receive a blessing from it. Let me remind you of what are some of the necessary ammunitions to defeat the Devil:

* Praying
* Studying God's Word
* Thinking good thoughts, singing and making melody in your heart to the Lord.

For anyone to receive any benefit from this book, they will have to do what this book recommends, and allow it to be a part of them. It will be good for them to read it over, and over again, so that it can be a part of your daily life, and then you will receive the full benefit from it.

I want to encourage you to do what Jesus, Job, and King David did, these are the three main character, of this Book who have gone through so much trouble. We can see what they did, they prayed, and God delivered them, he can also deliver you, if you continue to pray.

Prayer is the key for God to open the windows of Heaven, and to pour you out a blessing. It will be so abundant that you will have no room to keep it, so that you will be able to bless others.

Life is precious so we should desire to live every minute of it, and seek to live as long as we can.

Our life should be the most valued thing which the Creator has given to us.

We need to understand, that there is a Destroyer, who will do his best to try to kill us, but remember that Jesus Christ told us about the one, who is called the Devil, the Dragon, and Satan.

His work is to steal, to kill, and to destroy, but Jesus Christ says, that he comes to give life, and to give it more abundantly.

Jesus went to Hell, and he took back the power which the Devil had taken away from Adam and Eve, when they were in the Garden of Eden, and he brought it back to us so that we do not have to hide from God any more.

If we accept him today as our Saviour and let him into our heart, he will revive us and give us a new life and show us how to overcome the devils, who will tell you to take your life?

Please tell as many people as you can, about this Book, so that they too can receive the help that they need to receive, the Eternal life, which Jesus the Christ brought down from Heaven for us.

It is freely given without price, for whosoever will, the Bible in (Revelation 22) says 'let them take the water of life freely.'

God has got all that we need to overcome the Devil, the weapon of this great warfare, the (Word of God) which will destroy the works of the evil one; you just need to ask God for his help.

The Lord bless and keep you; the Lord make his face to shine upon you, and give you peace, now and forever.

However, I advice that in severe Cases Medical remediation is also necessary. We therefore recommend that Depression suffers who are on medication should consult their GP for confirmation of recovery before discarding any of their medications.

PART 2

How to Be a Good Parent

INTRODUCTION

The most precious gift which God has given to us, while we are here on Earth, is our children, whom we should look after and take care of.

We are instructed by God on how we are to bring up our children, but sad to say, we have neglected, even cast off, the teachings of God and replaced them with our own ideas. Because of that, we are reaping the fruits of our poor decisions.

When we look at what the children are doing, we see that so many of them already have a criminal record. Many of them indulge in binge-drinking and taking drugs. Some are killing one another. Depression is now sweeping through our society, especially our young people.

Many of them are mentally disturbed and/or commit suicide by taking an overdose of drugs, hanging themselves, self-mutilation or other methods. What a mess we are in! Where can we get help? We need to get back to God's way of bringing up our children.

The Bible, God's Word to us, is for every generation until Jesus returns. In it, clearly set out, are the ways in which we are to guide and instruct our children. This is for all nations, of every colour and race.

I think that we need to return to the old ways of following God's Word so that he can help us in these evil and violent days. We need to get back into the churches, where the people of God are, and seek him for the answers to our troubled world. Jesus says,

'Upon this rock, I will build my Church, and the gates of Hell, shall not prevail against it' (St Matthew.16:18KJV).

The devil will destroy everything that is on earth, except the Church, because Jesus's words must stand forever.

He says in (St Matthew 24:35KJV

"Heaven and Earth shall pass away, but my words shall not pass away."

All that he has told us will happen is coming true, to the letter.

Jesus has given us authority to fight against the devil. He has also given his angels the power to deliver the souls who are captured and bound in prison and to set them free to follow him.

Our children are precious souls whom we need to care for, guide, instruct and train up in the way they are to go, according to God's Word. When we have done our best in bringing up our children, and they still go astray, we need to constantly pray for them. Never give up; keep trusting in God. He will bring them back, and your prayers will be answered. They may go astray for many years, but sooner or later they will return to his fold. We need to believe that God is able to do much more than we think or ask.

We read of a man name Job in the Bible who offered sacrifice continually for his children. He did this just in case his sons had sinned and cursed God in their heart! Then one day the devil killed all ten of his children. Job did not weep; he began to worship God and said these famous words: 'The Lord gives, and the Lord takes away. Blessed be the name of the Lord'.

CHAPTER 1

What Is the Duty of Parents to Their Children?

(Psalm 127:1KJV) says,
"Except the Lord builds the house, they labour in vain that build it: Except the Lord keep the City, the watchman waketh but in vain".

I gather, then, that the Lord is interested in the building of our homes and in the keeping of our cities. Why is the Lord concerned about the building of our homes?

Because when the home is stable and functioning in the right way, it is a blessing to the nation.

We have seen the dysfunctional and broken homes, how great a problem which it is causing around the world.

(Psalm 127KJV)
"Lo, children are an heritage of the Lord: and the fruit of the womb, is his reward. As arrows are in the hand of a mighty man, so are children of the youth. Happy is the man that hath his quiver full of them: they shall not be ashamed, but they shall speak with the enemy in the gate".

The psalmist, King David, recognises the value of children, and he acknowledges that they come from God and are a gift for the hard work the parent has done. What would the world be like without children?

There would be no one to continue to be fruitful and multiply, as the Creator commanded us.

When a child is born, the parents should give thanks to God for that child, and when the child begins to grow, they should present the child in the house of God to be blessed by the people who represent God in his house.

(Proverbs 22:6KJV) says,
'Train up the child in the way that he should go: and when he is old, he will not depart from it."

Children should be taught about their Heavenly origin, and they should be taught about God and why they are here. They should be taught about Creation, which the Bible tells us about in Genesis chapter 1, and 2,

Training should begin from the child's first year of life, and it should continue until that child is fully grown and can provide for him- or herself.

They should be taught that God is a Spirit. He is invisible like the air which we breathe, or the wind which is all around us.

Let me take this privilege to teach the people of the world, the reason why we are here.

We are here to choose where we will live in the next life. This life which we are now living is a short one. We are allotted by God seventy years and he says that we may live longer, by reason of strength, but no matter how long we live we have to die.

God has given us the choice to accept Jesus Christ as our Saviour and receive everlasting life of happiness and joy with him in Paradise, (his kingdom), or refuse to follow him and spend everlasting life with the Devil in hell and then at the judgement in the lake of fire, as Jesus states in (St Matthew 25:41KJV)

They should be taught how to work while at home so that, when they are of age, they will be ready to take a job and take responsibility for themselves in the community. This way it will not be strange to them when they have to face the hard facts of life.

Home should be a training ground, where children are taught about the real world. They should be taught that the television shows and video games are make-believe that those men and women are acting.

It is also the parent's duty to monitor what their children watch on television and online, because there are many evil people who will lead their children astray. It is both parents' duty to teach their children about what they will face in the world.

One of the first things that children should be taught is to respect their:

Parents, themselves, authorities of the country, where they live, their elders, and the laws of the land. This teaching is vital for their well-being, that they may be a blessing and not a terror, to the nation and community where they are living.

It is so sad to see some of the children today who have no respect for anyone. They break the law, even to the point of killing each other, taking drugs, filling up the prisons, joining gangs, and terrorising people.

What can we do to stem the violence, which some of our young people are causing today?

I believe that our prisons should be a place of training so that when offenders are released, they will be skilled men and women able to get stable jobs.

If they were not trained at home, then the prisons should be able to do the training, which is necessary for them.

In the Book of Proverbs it says that children left to themselves will bring their parents to shame, but a wise son makes a glad Father.

How can our children be wise? They need to be taught so that they will learn how to be wise. If they are not instructed, they will not know right from wrong.

Imagine that on the roads there were: no instructions, no signs, no speed limits, and no warnings of dangers ahead. How would we manage to drive? We would not know where to go! Of course, they put up signs for us to follow. Just as these signs are needed for us to reach our destination safely, there should be constant training for children to follow, so they can arrive safely where they need to go.

CHAPTER 2

The Duty of Fathers

Fathers have a duty to see that their children are cared for and are brought up in the way that the God of heaven and earth has laid down. This is for their well-being that they will not be like wild horses, under no control.

(Ephesian 6:4KJV) says,
"And, ye fathers, provoke not your children to wrath: but bring them up in the nurture and admonition of the Lord".

The Bible is telling fathers not to provoke their children to anger. Rather, it says that fathers should bring up their children by nurturing them and admonishing them about the Lord.

The father has a vital role in the home. His duty is to instruct his children about the dangers that they will face daily when they grow up.

Nurture and admonition—what do these words mean? The Scriptures are comparing children to young plants, which a gardener places in his garden. He has to: water it, fertilise it, and weed the surrounding area of other plants that would steal moisture and nutrients.

When the gardener does the work of caring for the garden, we can then see the beautiful flowers. So it will be when a father nurtures his children by caring for them and instructing them. You will then see a beautiful family: husband, wife, and children, and they will then be a blessing to their community.

The Scriptures say that fathers should be there to help their children when they are young and to see to it that they don't grow like wild animals, or wild plants. There should be constant nurturing that only fathers can give.

Children should be taught discipline in the home because the home is the first place which God has given authority.

(Ephesians 6:1–3KJV) says,

"Children, obey your parents in the Lord: for this is right. Honour thy father and thy mother; which is the first commandment with promise; that it may be well with thee, and that thou may live long on the earth." The Bible say that God promise to give our children long life if they obey this commandment. Sad to see that the parents does not teach their children or bring their children to the church so that we can teach them this commandment.

What is the promise?

It is God promising you that he will allow you to live a long life. When the killer, the Devil comes to kill you, God will defend you, because you honour your parents.

I believe that many of our young people who have been killed, in various ways, by gun-men, knife-men, suicide, by drug over dose, also by many horrible fatal road accident.

God could not defend them when death came to take them to the next life, because he cannot go against his Word, which says if any one curse their parents, let them die the death. In the days of the Ten

Commandments if any one curse their Parents the people would stone those wicked children, but since Jesus brought the new Commandment he told us to forgive, but the devil who is the death angel will oppose God and demand that that child must be killed.

Fathers, we need to teach our children God's Word. I encourage you to make the greatest investment that you will ever make in your life, to buy a Bible and teach it to your children. 'Why the Bible?' you may ask. Because it is God's Word to all human beings; it transcends all religious barriers, and it is for all Nations.

You may say,' I have my own Religion,' but you need to know that God is looking for a relationship with you. Your religious books are good, but the Bible teaches us of: the beginning, the present, and the future. No other book comes close to it. It has advice for every situation that we face in life. Daily we struggle to find answers to our problems, not knowing that God has given us the answers in his Book.

The things written in it over four thousand years ago, are coming through which are so clearly seen in our time: the violence, the pollution, the corruption. We are seeing great signs and wonders, which Jesus spoke about, and he said that when we see these signs, he is coming soon. He said that we should stand in the Holy place. Where is the Holy place? It is the house of God which we have built and consecrated to gather for corporate worship. The Word of God also say that we should not forsake the assembling of ourselves together. But we should gather more often especially when we see the day of his return approaching.

Let us look at Admonition

This is the instruction and guidance which we were given by God to pass on to our children which he has given, as a gift for us to keep and care for them until they are of age.

(Proverbs 4:1–24KJV) sets out some of the instruction which we should give to our children:

1 "Hear, ye children, the instruction of a father, and attend to know understanding.

2 For I give you good doctrine, forsake you not my law.

3 For I was my father's son, tender and only beloved in the sight of my mother.

4 He taught me also, and said unto me, let thine heart retain my words: keep my commandments, and live.

5 Get wisdom, get understanding: forget it not; neither decline from the words of my mouth.

6 Forsake her not, and she shall preserve thee: Love her, and she shall keep thee.

7 Wisdom is the principal thing; therefore get Wisdom: and with all thy getting get understanding.

8 Exalt her, and she shall promote thee: she shall bring thee to honour, when thou dost embrace her.

9 She shall give to thine head an ornament of grace: a crown of glory shall she deliver to thee.

10 Hear, O my son, and receive my sayings; and the years of thy life shall be many.

11 I have taught thee in the way of wisdom; I have led thee in right paths. 12 When thou goest thy steps shall not be straitened; and when thou runnest, thou shall not stumble.

13 Take fast hold of instruction; let her not go: keep her; for she is thy life.

14 Enter not into path of the wicked, and go not in the way of evil men.

15 Avoid it, pass not by it, turn from it, and pass away.

16 For they sleep not, except they have done some mischief; and their sleep is taken away, unless they cause some to fall.

17 For they eat the bread of wickedness, and drink the wine of violence.

18 But the path of the just is as the shining light, that shines more and more, unto the perfect day.

19 The way of the wicked is as darkness: they know not at what they stumble.

20 My son, attain to my words; incline thine ear unto my sayings.

21 Let them not depart from thine eyes; keep them in the midst of thy heart.

22 For they are life to those that find them, and health, to all their flesh.

23 Keep thy heart with all diligence; for out of it are the issues of life.

24 Put away from thee a forward mouth, and perverse lips put far from thee."

When we read the words of Solomon (the son of King David) in Proverbs, Ecclesiastes, and the Songs of Solomon, we can see why God said that David was a man after his own heart. The king instructed his son, who would be king after his death, and we now have these words to guide us in all generations.

Remember, God has instructed us in the way that we are to bring up our children, but we have turned away from his words. We have taken our children out of the House of God and we refuse to bring them back no matter how the preachers encourage us. Jesus says to the people in his day that they should not stop the little children from coming to him, for of such is the kingdom of God.

The mothers had brought their little children to Christ for him to bless them, but the disciples tried to turn them away. The Bible declares that when Jesus saw it, he was very displeased, and he rebuked them. Then he took the children into his arms and blessed them.

Let me ask you this question: 'Have you taken your children to the House of God to be blessed?' or are you saying that you and your children do not need the blessing of God. You can be blessed at any age, even when you are an adult. God will bless you at any age; you are never too old! He says that age is nothing to him, we are always his little children when we come to him.

Rules in the home for guiding children

There should be rules in the home, rules which will give guidance to children when they are growing up. If there are no rules, the children will be out of control, and the Devil will take control and break up your home.

God has laid down the rules for us to follow so that we can have stable homes. It is very sad to see our children rejecting the way of the Lord and refusing to change so that the Lord can bless us. Let us get back to the old way of following the teachings of Jesus Christ so that there can be a change in our society.

Fathers are given the responsibility of instructing their children so that they will be a blessing to their community, but some fathers have abandoned their children and their duty to God. I repeat, (Proverb22:6KJV) says,

"Train up the Child in the way he should go: and when he is old, he will not depart from it."

The Proverb says he, but that does not mean that we should not train the girls also.

According to the Bible, it should be a constant training process for all children, until they reach the age of maturity. Fathers, start the training that your children need right now. If you have neglected to train them, it is better to start late than never.

It is such a wonderful blessing when you have done the right training as a father, to see your children grow up and are a blessing to their society.

CHAPTER 3

The Duty of a Mother

I have seen so many women today struggling to bring up their children alone because the fathers have deserted them and the children.

I have seen so many mothers who desire to do the best for the family, but the father doesn't care. They have to scrimp and save to buy a home with no help from the father.

Those women should be helped by the authorities.

I believe that when a mother decides to stay at home and look after her children, there should be financial help given to them by the Government so that they can accomplish this Devine task. In this way we can address the gap between the rich and the poor.

For hundreds of years, we have had the trickle-down process from the rich to the poor. It is time for it to flow down, especially to those women who are doing a wonderful work of bringing up their children at home.

A mother who has chosen to look after the family at home has chosen a good career. She will be grooming the ones who may be the heads of industry, who may hold vital and important jobs in the future. Those children might grow up to be the President or a Prime Minister, of a country so, ladies, your work of caring for the family should not be looked upon as inferior to the work outside the home in Business.

Ladies, let me encourage you: If you decide to be a homemaker, it is a hard job. You are entrusted with the lives of precious souls, so do the best that you can. You may have many sleepless nights, much heartache, but when they are grown up and begin to excel in their chosen careers, it will be rewarding to see all of your hard work bearing fruit.

You may have to do without in order to see your children progress. Many of our women are facing severe hardship, depression, anxieties, and worries for the welfare of their children, especially in such a violent times as we are living in today. Many mothers are watching their children slaughtered on the roads.

Some of our mothers have to go to food banks to get food for their children to survive. It is a shame on this country which has ruled many other nations and told us that justice needs to be seen done. How can this country preside over this unjust system which allows our mothers to be in such great needs for them and their children?

Where is the justice for these mothers? It is so sad to say that this is a problem in which many of our young, single mothers in the world are facing.

Many fathers have abandoned their duty of looking after their children, and they are going around from one woman to another without worrying about the consequences that they are leaving behind. We need to educate our young men about the duty of being a father so that they will help with the upbringing of the children.

There are so many broken homes, without a father to train up the children, and this is part of the reason why there is so much violence in our societies and cities of the world.

We need to understand that a woman's duty is to help the man to run the home. They have joint responsibilities to care for, and bring up, the children. The man should be able to wash, cook, and do housework so that the woman is not a slave in the house.

Remember the old proverb that, 'the horse is not too good to carry its own grass,' meaning that the children is not too good to help in the home.

If the father can afford to employ someone to help the mother, then he should do so, to take the burden off the mother.

Children should be taught to help with the work in the home: wash the dishes, clean the floor, and take out the rubbish. They should not leave their clothes on the floor for their mother to pick up. They should put their clothes in the proper place to be washed instead, and they should be taught how to wash clothes.

Mothers, you are not a slave for your family in the house. You are to teach the family that helping hands make light work. This teaching is vital so that when your children grow up, they will be ready to work for their daily bread. I have seen many mothers who refuse to allow their children to help them in the kitchen. Then they became stressed out from the work of providing food for the family. Don't turn them out! They are there to learn how to cook and to give you a helping hand. One day they will learn. Be patient with them; you did not learn overnight, so don't expect them to.

Also, mothers, you need to train up your sons as well as your daughters to do housework. And remember, housework is never done. It needs daily looking after, so teach them to be clean and tidy. Teach them to wash their hands regularly, to cut and clean their nails because germs can flourish in their dirty nails. You should teach them Hygiene. In the 19/50ties and 19/60ties this was a part of the school curriculum. Children would be taught how to be clean.

Women, you need to teach your man that he needs to work in the home as well—if his mother did not teach him. You need to teach and train him. Let him know that you need his help in the home, even if you are at home all day with the children. Let him know that it is not easy work to keep the family fed and clean daily. Remember, you are not there to wait on them, hand and foot, as the old saying goes. If anyone in the family sees something that needs to be done, that person should do it.

Mothers since you are in charge of the house, you have the right to give each person specific duties in the home, else you will be killing yourself. Be wise. The Proverb says that a wise woman builds her house, but the foolish breaks it down with her hands.

Just imagine a young mother with four children, fourteen years and under, who has to be both father and mother for them; it can be heart-breaking. Having to work part-time; taking her children to school seven miles away and bringing them back each day; and cooking, washing, and cleaning daily—it's unthinkable for one person.

A good woman in the home is the most precious asset, for both the man and the family. The wise man King Solomon says.

(Proverbs 31:10–31KJV)
"Who can find a virtuous woman?
For her price is far above rubies.
11 The heart of her husband doth safely trust in her, so that he shall have no need of spoils.
12 She will do him good and not evil all the days of her life.
13 She seeketh wool, and flax, and worketh willingly with her hands.
14 She is like the merchant's ships; she bringeth her food from afar.
15 She riseth also while it is yet night, and giveth meat to her household, and a portion to her maidens.
16 She considers a field, and buys it: with the fruit of her hands she planteth a vineyard.

17 She girdeth her loins with strength, and strengtheneth her arms.

18 She perceiveth that her merchandise is good: her candle goeth not out by night.

19 She layeth her hands to the spindle, and her hands hold the distaff.

20 She stretcheth out her hand to the poor; yea, she reacheth fourth her hands to the needy.

21 She is not afraid of the snow for her household: for all her household are clothed with scarlet.

22 She maketh herself covering of tapestry; her clothing is silk and purple. 23 Her husband is known in the gates, when he sitteth among the elders of the land.

24 She maketh fine linen, and selleth it; and delivereth girdles unto the merchants.

25 Strength and honour are her clothing; and she shall rejoice in time to come.

26 She openeth her mouth with wisdom; and in her tongue is the law of kindness.

27 She looketh well to the ways of her household, and eateth not the bread of idleness.

28 Her children arise up, and called her blessed; her husband also, and he praiseth her.

29 Many daughters have done virtuously, but you excel them all.

30 Favour is deceitful, and beauty is vain: but a woman that feareth the Lord, she shall be praised.

31 Give her of the fruit of her hands; and let her own works praised her in the gates."

Rev. Michael Walker

These are the words of the wisest man, King Solomon, even though he said that he could not understand a woman.

When we see so many women struggling to bring up children alone, we should lift our hats to them and help them in any way we can.

CHAPTER 4

The Duty of Grandparents

Grandparents can be a vital help to their grandchildren. They should be involved in the bringing up of their offspring.

Parents should seek advice and help if the children grandparents are alive. Then also, when parents cannot cope, then grandparents (if they're healthy and have the accommodations) should take the children for a while until things are sorted out. Then the children can be returned home. If things cannot be put right at home, then the children should stay with their grandparents until they are fully grown.

I can remember when I was about five years old, in Jamaica; my father went to the USA on a six months contract. My mother could not cope alone with five children, so I was sent to my grandparents. They were willing to keep me, but when my dad returned, I returned home to see him and I did not return to live with my grandparents. Although they had loved and cared for me, I chose to be with my parents.

Grandparents should be encouraged to help, to council their grandchildren and great-grandchildren. There should be times set apart at weekends, when they can gather as a family, have a meal, and talk with each other.

This will allow the grandchildren to know and appreciate that there is someone who also loves them and cares for them. Let's get back to the old ways of caring for each other, and being a part of, a family.

Grandparents should teach their children not to allow the grandchildren to take side with one parent over the other. They should respect Daddy and Mummy equally. Children should see parents in unity.

If a child asks to sleep at a friend's house for the night, the parents should consult with each other. Neither parent should overturn a decision without discussing it. If a decision *is* changed, the first parent should then share that change with the children rather than having one parent saying 'no' and the other saying 'yes'.

Children will exploit our disunity if they think that they can get away with it, but, for their good, there should be unity between parents. Never quarrel in their presence. If there is any disagreement, then parents should sort it out together but not in front of the children. They should not be involved in open parental disagreements.

Why?

That can affect them in the time when they have their own companion and have to bring up their own children.

If they were brought up to be discreet and not to be a brawler then they will bring up their children in the same way.

CHAPTER 5

Advice to Women

It is believed that women of old were wiser than the women of today. Those wise women, tested the men to see if they were runners or stayers. They would say to the man with whom they were going out that I am an expensive woman, which meant your hands must be free to spend money on me. If the man was stingy, and mean he would back off.

I believe that the women of today need to get back to the old ways, for their own good. Some men today do not want the responsibility of bringing up even their own children. They just want to have a good time by going from one woman to another, then leaving them to cope with any children, on their own.

In the olden days, there was a time of courtship before any sexual relationship began. This was another of the ways that women tested men to see if they were genuine or just wanted a loose relationship.

Those women would wait for the man to open the door of a car to help her in, and then drive her to their destination. She would again wait until he came around and opened the door.

The man was expected to wine and dine her at a restaurant or take her to the cinema before bringing her home, *safely* to her door. He might kiss her on the hand or cheek and say good night, and that would be all.

Rev. Michael Walker

A good man or woman would not expect a sexual relationship until they are sure that this was the one they wanted to marry and raise a family with.

These days it seems that many of our young men just want to go to bed with as many women as they can. If they have children, they are not prepared to take the responsibility for them.

Wise up, women! Why do you let yourself be used in this way? It is time for women to take a stand and say as the Good Book says '***no sex before marriage.***'

Women, you need to ask the man if he knows what he is getting into—that having a sexual relationship will bring children, and children need to be taken care of. Find out if he is willing to take that responsibility. If he is not willing, then let him walk. It is better to lose him at this stage than when you have two or three children to care for, and then you end up with depression, maybe even contemplating suicide.

CHAPTER 6

Advice to Fathers

Fathers, you need to do the work of a Godly father. You should be the minister of your family, the one who leads and guides them in the right way. Bringing up a child takes time, hard work, and patience.

A father should be willing to go to his children's school for events and teacher's meetings also to see their works and to discuss with the teachers his children's educational progress.

This is a must!

He and the teachers should work in harmony for the good of the children.

Never oppose the teacher in the presence of your child, even if the teacher is in the wrong. If there is a disagreement, then discuss it with the teacher alone. This will show the child that they must respect the teacher's authority.

I remember a teacher and I were once talking about discipline in school, and she told me about the problems she has when a parent has to be called in. She reported that many of our young people are abusive, and they know they can abuse teachers and get away with it.

Let me remind all parents that the teacher is there for the education of your child. You need to work together.

Fathers, let me give you some sound advice: You should be the role model for your children. God has ordained you as the first authority the children has, and they are a part of you. Every rapist, murderer, prostitute, fraudster, drug runner, gunman, and bomber was first someone's child. Maybe if they had gotten a proper upbringing, they would never have allowed the devil to use them for these evil deeds. You may say, 'I have brought up my children in the right way, but they turned out bad!' Then your duty is to constantly pray for them, that God will change them.

If you are a father who has deserted your children, please reconnect with them, for your own good and theirs.

Why?

You may ask. Well, one day you must give an account to the heavenly Father for the way that you have neglected your duty to your children.

CHAPTER 7

Prisons should be Places of Training

Because many fathers have abandoned their children—and many of our homes are without training and instruction—some of our children get into trouble with the law. For this reason, there should be a training program in all prisons—so that when offenders are released, they will be well-trained tradespeople.

What type of training should prisons provide?

There should be training on: car mechanics and bodywork, carpentry, plumbing, electrics, electronics, bricklaying, plaster work, and also degree courses for those who desire further education. This will enable them when they are released, to be skilled, or well educated people.

The Bible says that, if a man does not work, neither should he eat. Furthermore, if we can't find work for people to do, the old proverb says that, 'the devil will find work for idle hands to do,' and *his* work is stealing killing and destroying the lives of our young people.

In the olden days, after the allotted time of schooling, youth would have to go and learn a trade if they were not going into higher education. Their parents would see to that. They would ask a tradesperson to teach their children, even if they had to pay.

What has gone wrong today that so many of our young people are walking the streets, being idle, joining gangs, terrorising people, and filling up the prisons? After they are released, into the society they end up back in prison because they still don't have something healthier to do.

Something must be done, and done ***now***, to save our young generation from the hands of the Devil. Remember what Jesus says, the devil comes to steal, to kill, and to destroy, but he Jesus came to give life abundantly.

Where are the wise leaders of today who will guide our people? Are there no longer any wise men and women who can guide our leaders? Are they just looking out for themselves, to selfishly get all they can?

When I hear about the exorbitant wages many of our chief executives are getting, I wonder if they have no conscience. Do they not care for people who are at the lower end of the pay scale? The Bible tells us—the ministers of God, to whom he has given a charge—that we should tell the rich to give to the poor.

(1 Timothy 6:17–19 KJV)
"Charge them are rich in this World, that they be not high minded, nor trust in uncertain riches, but in the living God, who gives us richly all things to enjoy;

18 That they do good, that they be rich in good works, ready to distribute, willing to communicate;

19 Laying up in store for themselves a good foundation against the time to come, that they may lay hold on eternal life."

The wealth of the nations is not solely for the elite or those who have been well educated; it should be fairly distributed. Many of our CEO's need to forgo their pay rise for a few years so that those who are at the bottom of the pay scale can catch up. If they don't, let me refer them to the message of Jesus Christ: 'What shall it profit a man if he

God's Advice to the Nations of the World

gains the whole world but loses his one soul, or what will a man give in exchange for his soul?'

Let me advise you, then: Don't sell your soul for money. It will not profit you when you have to cross to the other side. Death will take you, sooner or later, to meet your Maker, and money will not help you then, so be generous to others. Give so that you will receive the gift of eternal life when you return to your Maker.

CHAPTER 8

Drug Abuse

Children should be taught about drug abuse and the dangers of it to their health. They should be taught that the safest way is to abstain from taking drugs altogether. It will seem good, but it bites as a serpent does, and it can destroy their lives and eventually kill them.

After teaching them the dangers, we should know that they might ignore our advice and try to experiment. This shouldn't come as a surprise, given that God gave Adam and Eve one prohibition and they disobeyed, plunging the world into chaos. ***But God, our loving Father, did not kill them or throw them in prison. Instead, He clothed them and began to educate and support them, as he has been doing for us ever since.***

When God created the herbs of the field, he said that it was for food and that all he created was good. The problem is that people have abused it.

Now, we may wonder, is there any way to stop the wide-scale drug abuse going on around the world?

We have tried for decades to stop the importing of drugs, and it does not work. We have put multiple policing bodies on the task, and they have not made any progress toward stopping it from flooding the world.

Our people are being destroyed. Many young lives are cut short by drug-related killings. How many more must die before we do something positive to stop the abuse? You may ask what we can do.

God, in his wisdom, has ordained governments to stop us from excess and from destroying ourselves. If there were no government or law, anarchy would prevail.

Let us consider what can governments do to stop the abuse of drugs? You may say that they have already formed laws against the dissemination of drugs, but this could be the problem. Think about the time of the prohibition of alcohol in the United States, when men like Al Capone and his gang could terrorise the people of Chicago. But as soon as they stopped the prohibition, the killing also stopped.

I think that it is time for world governments to come together and discuss how to take drugs out of the hands of criminals and instead control them so that those who need these herbs could be helped, supported, and educated. Putting drug users in prison and criminalising them will never stop the abuse because they can get the drugs in prison.

Drug money laundering could be stopped at once. The funds that we use to try to stop drugs from coming into the country could be used instead to provide help for the needy. Let us look at how this could be done. Governments could buy the product from those who produce it, use what is needed for medication, and destroy what is not needed. They could create a legally run rehabilitation system which could prescribe, sell, and treat those who need to be treated. That system would create jobs for doctors and nurses, and would be funded by the sale of those drugs.

Let me ask a question. What does it cost the government today? They cannot fully fund the National Health Service, (NHS) because of the pressures that are being put on it from treating people who have drug-related illnesses.

Some may say this cannot work.

We read that Portugal had to make the decision in 2001 to decriminalise the use of drugs, because their country was being destroyed by the prohibition. So far it is working.

'Why is it then that the other nations are not following their example? 'Is there a hidden agenda which nobody knows about?

What we have done for the last one hundred years has not worked. Should we continue using our failing system, or should we seek another way?

Prohibition did not work in the Garden of Eden, nor did it work with the Ten Commandments. God said he found fault with it, so he took it away and brought in a New Covenant, with better promises, and this way is to love, support, and educate. If prohibition did not work with God, how can it work with us, who have all sinned and come short of God's glory?

Let us look at Jesus' words written in the Holy Scriptures.

(St Matthew 28:18–20KJV)

18'And Jesus came and spake onto them, saying, All power is given unto me in heaven and in earth.

19 Go ye therefore and teach all nations, baptising them in the name of the Father, and of the Son, and of the Holy Ghost:

20 Teaching them to observe all things whatsoever I have commanded you: and lo, I am with you alway, even unto the end of the world."

That command applies to us, his disciples, who are following his teachings today, but it seems that we are teaching only ourselves and do not worry about teaching the Nations.

When Jesus was here, the Bible says that multitudes followed him, and his disciples told him to send them away to buy their own food. However, he said he could not send them away hungry, so he miraculously fed them with five loves and two fishes, even though there were about five thousand men, plus women and children.

Jesus is concerned about our temporal and our spiritual life, but are we also concerned about each other's? Or are we just concerned about number one-me only? It is time for us to change, for he is coming very soon, to take control of the Earth.

CONCLUSION

It is so sad to see what is happening to our children and youth today. Many of them have no hope for the future, nor many job prospects. Some will never be able to own a house because the price of housing is so high. People have speculated in houses, so the cost has gone through the roof.

The things necessary for life, like the commodity, which we need for food, such as Cocoa, Wheat, and Soya Beans, is gambled on in the stock exchange so that the rich get richer and the poor get poorer. What can we do to address this evil, which has led us astray and caused these problems in our society?

The problem is that Governments are not governing as God designed them to. They allow market forces to dictate, and that is not God's way. If any country has no government, then anarchy will prevail, along with lawlessness and evil will.

God has designed things such that, in all walks of life, there must be rules. If we let market forces dictate the economy, then that is anarchy. This is why the Nations of the world are in distress and have to borrow to keep their economy going.

How is it that 10% per cent of the world's population owns more than 50% per cent of the wealth? When we look at the Word of God, we can see that it foretells this so accurately; it tells us what will happen in the last days.

Rev. Michael Walker

(St Luke 21:25KJV)

"And there shall be signs in the sun, and in the moon, and in the stars; and upon the earth distress of nations, with perplexity; the sea and the waves roaring."

When we look at the situation of the world today, we are in a sad state.

All the nations have to borrow to keep their economies going, and many of the nations are facing the heavy hand of austerity to keep their country from bankruptcy.

Look at what is happening in our times. We see a country like Greece, the third greatest superpower of the olden days (BC), trying to keep from going into bankruptcy by getting loans. We need to get back to God's way. He says that the things of the Earth are for all the people to profit. If we allow speculators to have no rules, then we are saying that we know more than God. But look! What is happening to our nations today, it is not good—that the governments should preside over so many years of austerity?

Here is what needs to be put in place soon so that we can advance in the twenty-first century. When children finish schooling, there should be no dole money given to them, but they should receive training allowances. The allowance should be given to employers, to supplement the wages of the trainee until their training is over. This should be done in such a way that the youth would want to learn a trade rather than to get job-seekers allowance. Many of our youths do not want to go into higher education, and they should go into training immediately, as soon they finish their childhood education. All employers should be encouraged to take on trainees so that our young people become well trained,

Were the people of olden times wiser than the people of today? I think not, but they used common sense, which we are not using today, and our children are joining gangs and working for the devil. Who will be the bold ones who will stand up and say our children need something better than what they are getting? May the God of heaven help us if we neglect the training of our children? Jesus says that some children will rise up against their parents and will cause some to be put to death in the last days. So let us take heed and do what is right, because we are in the last days now.

PART 3

How to deal with Pollution

INTRODUCTION

Pollution, the scourge of the Earth- what can we do to stop this horrible problem which all the Nations are facing today? We have read in the Scriptures that when Jesus rose from the dead, he told his disciples that he was the one who was dead, and now he is alive forever more. He said that he has all power in heaven and on Earth. He instructed them to go and teach the nations. Jesus told us that he gives us the authority to teach all the nations of the world.

(Matt. 28:18–20, KJV)

18 And Jesus came and spake unto them, saying, 'All Power is given unto me in Heaven and in Earth.

19 Go ye therefore, and teach all nations, baptising them in the name of the Father, and of the Son, and of the Holy Ghost:

20 Teaching them to observe all things whatsoever I have commanded you: And lo, I am with you alway even unto the end of the world.'

We today, who are followers of the teachings of Jesus Christ are his disciples. I will therefore do my best to teach my fellow men-to let them know that we have a duty to look after the environment, which God has entrusted to our care. Many preachers, whom God gave the authority to teach the Nations, have neglected to do the work of teaching about the effects of a polluted environment.

Rev. Michael Walker

Let us take a long, hard look at the destruction of our environment and what can we do, at this stage, to stop or slow down the destruction we are causing. There are several measures we can put into operation if we are bold enough to do so, especially when it comes to the pollution caused by motor vehicles. I will set out some common-sense measures. If our leaders are brave and determined enough to take this advice, we can begin to address some of these problems.

We can see the devastation of our planet. It will take one bold nation to start radical action in their part of the world so that other nations can follow.

Let us, in the United Kingdom, be that radical nation and show the way. The UK is a little Island, but it has ruled many countries that are many times larger than it. It has ruled over a third of the world. Once, the saying was that the sun never went down on the British Empire. No other empire could make that claim. They have stood for justice across the world; this phrase has been used in our Courts since 1924, Justice must be seen to be done.

When they had to stand up against the tyranny of Hitler, they refused to surrender in the face of near defeat. They have won two world wars and set many nations free. What the world needs today is a nation to show the way, to tackle pollution, which is destroying the Earth.

Let us take the mantle again, as we did in the days of ending slavery, when it was outlawed in London. The rest of Europe was continuing to trade in slaves, yet the UK stepped forward and fought to stop the trade in human cargo. They eventually forced Europe, Africa, and the Middle East to end the slave trade. Against all odds, the Royal Navy, given two ships to accomplish the almost impossible task of patrolling the seas and capturing slave ships, did so with distinction, honour, and determination. This is the willpower which is needed to tackle pollution today.

Let us remember that when God put Adam and Eve in the Garden of Eden, he commanded them to 'keep it'. (Gen 2:15 KJV) I believe that if we begin a radical cleaning up of our environment, God will help us.

I remember when we came from the West Indies to the UK, in the 1950s and '60s; the smog was so bad that it was harming people. The government decided to stop the burning of coal. That action worked well then, and today we need to take some equally drastic actions to clean up our environment.

One of our main problems which we are facing today is pollution from the motor vehicles. If we can solve this, I believe that we can have a beautiful Earth again.

When I hear that our seas are full of plastic from our washing machines, these appliances should then be fitted with filters so that no small particles from the clothes escape into the water system. This could be done to all our existing machines at a minimal cost.

On all our rivers, there should be a barrier, built of mesh wire, at the end where it meets the sea, to prevent plastics from entering the sea, and it should be cleaned regularly. There should be a furnace to burn all the rubbish that we have used and the waste which we are creating. Fire consumes. It is not good that we are piling up all the rubbish that we have created, and are creating daily.

In these days of ever increasing house prices, it would be good if we could globally find a way to recycle our own plastics, to use it to help in the building of affordable housing.

The Bible tells us that when Jesus rose from the dead, the burial clothes in which he was buried were folded and put in their proper place, separate from each other. I gather from that, that God is clean, and he expects us to clean up the pure environment which he gave us.

Let us not procrastinate any longer in putting the necessary resources and manpower into cleaning up our mess, which we have caused. Let us not be like the lazy man who is sleeping with rubbish in his house and will not take the time to clean it. Are we too lazy to start cleaning up our environment?

We should employ people to clean up the environment. Plastics bags, bottles, cups, and plates should be gathered and burned. That would cause less pollution than to leave them lying around, damaging the food chains. A partially refundable charge should be placed on these plastics, refunded when anyone brings them back. This has been done in numerous places on bottles, so why can't it be done here and now on a wider range of items? The un-refunded part of the charge could go to the local authority to help to defray the cost of cleaning up the environment. These are simple common-sense measures that we should adopt to protect our environment.

CHAPTER 1

How to Fix Our Polluted Environment

Jesus Christ, the creator of heaven and Earth, gave us a great commission when he was leaving this realm; he told us that all power was given to him, in heaven and on Earth (Matt. 28, KJV). He said that we should teach all the nations. I hope that this book will be a good teaching tool for the nations of the world.

Let us look back, at the beginning of Creation. God told Adam, whom he had created, that his duty was to dress the garden of Eden, and he was instructed to keep it clean, which means that he should look after his environment:

(Genesis 2: 8, 15 KJV)

8 'And the Lord God planted a garden eastward in Eden; and there he put the man whom he had formed.

15 And the Lord God took the man, and put him into the garden of Eden to dress and to keep it.'

When we look at God's specific details, we can see that Adam was instructed to keep the garden- his home, clean and tidy. He was commanded to dress it, which means he should look after it.

There was only one prohibition in the garden: Adam was commanded not to eat of the tree in the midst of the garden, the tree of knowledge of good and evil. He was told not to touch it, but as soon as he disobeyed and ate of the tree which he already knew not to even touch, he realised that he was naked. He began to hide from God. When God called to him, he was afraid because he had lost his power to stand in God's presence. After God confronted him, he was cast out of the garden, and he was told that consequently, because of his disobedience, he was now left to fend for himself—to till the ground and to plant his own food (Gen 3 KJV). He would have to sweat for his daily bread. We have seen the effects of Adam's and Eve's disobedience.

We should learn from what happened to Adam and Eve, but, sad to say, we are so stubborn that we refuse to learn from the past. We are now facing global pollution on a large scale, which is destroying our environment and the lives of people. Worse, we seem to be helpless in even knowing what to do. The Bible has stated exactly what we should do, but, because we have gone astray from the Word of God, we are suffering great distress.

Now we might ask ourselves the question; where, or how, can we find the answer? Let us go back to the Word of God. It tells us that when we have strayed too far, we should seek for the old path, and when we find it, we should follow it.

(Jeremiah 6:16–19 KJV) says,

16 'Thus saith the Lord, stand thee in the ways and see, and ask for the old paths, where is the good way. But they said, We will not walk therein.'

17 Also I set watchmen over you, saying, Harken to the sound of the trumpet. But they said, we will not harken.

18 Therefore hear ye nations, and know, O congregation, what is among them.

19 Here, O earth: behold, I will bring evil upon this people, even the fruit of their thoughts, because they have not harkened unto my words, nor to my law, but rejected it.'

God has always wanted the best for us, but we have settled for the worst, as the people in Jeremiah's days refused to heed God's instructions. I can see the stubborn will of today's people, who think that they are right and refuse to take instruction from anyone. We refuse to obey the Word of God; we refuse to go back to the old ways, where the good paths are.

Let me ask this question: How did the people of the olden days get it so right, and we, in the twenty-first century, are making so many mistakes in such an advanced time as this? If we refuse to obey the words of God, as spoken by men and women of God, we do so at our own peril.

As God's sons and daughters living in this polluted world, I wish that the nations would hear what we are saying to them and take our advice according to God's principles.

How can we find the old paths? We have long kept records of the past so that the generation coming after us can have a history of what we have done.

We need to find out how our ancestors planned their path. It is not shameful to admit that we have got it wrong and then try to take advice from our elders. If we ignore their guidance, however, we will destroy ourselves.

First let us look at the motor vehicle. It is one of the best means of transportation. When city planners were laying out streets, they planned for the time when the use of motor vehicles would increase. If we take a closer look at many roads, we notice that the developers had to leave room in the front of buildings and houses for the widening of the roads. Yet, today, planners have narrowed these roads and caused bottlenecks on major roads. These modern planners have blocked off many of the side roads and created one-way streets, causing traffic to stay on the major roads. These vehicles are putting out so much pollution, which is harming the environment and the people.

Because of this increase in pollution, great strain is put on the National Health Service, NHS to treat pollution-related sicknesses, like asthma. These sicknesses are getting worse. There is no one who can convince these city planners that it is their irresponsibility, why there is so much pollution.

How can we stop this bad planning? There should be a select committee, made up of national and local people, who would scrutinise these plans. They will need to have the power to force planners to widen roads where they can be widened. The motor vehicle needs to go from point A to point B in the shortest time possible (while still safe) to minimise time on the roads and thus, reduce the pollution.

Now let us look at the side roads. There should be width limits which will prevent Trucks, and large vehicles, from going through them, so that only cars, motor cycles, and Bikes can drive through these limits. That was the old system that planners used.

Why have we strayed from those plans when we have millions of cars on the roads today? We are not using common sense.

Today's road planners put great humps on the roads, at the cost of thousands of pounds each, and they are not effective in slowing down vehicles.

The money which the Councils are throwing away on humps could be put into the service of the community, to help the aged by giving them a better social care system. Also the funds saved from not putting humps on the roads, could help to keep the community charge low.

You may argue about what we should use to slow down traffic in built-up areas or around schools. When planners were building the

God's Advice to the Nations of the World

motorways in the old days, they put in calming measures. Let me try to describe those calming measures, they are like strips of concrete placed between the carriage way and the hard shoulder, so that when your vehicle needed to come off the carriage way onto the hard shoulder, those calming measures would slow the vehicle down. This type of calming measure could be put on the local roads instead of humps. It will be a better way of calming the traffic, and at a minimal cost.

If these calming measures are installed where schools are, and other places where the roads should be twenty, 20MPH, it could slow down the traffic far better than what we have at present.

Let us look at the positive action of one of our Councils in London. They removed all the humps off of the roads, and yet there has not been an increase in accidents. That is common sense in operation. The other councils should follow their example and stop throwing money away, which is needed for the upkeep of their communities. That money could go to help social services and pensioners.

The greatest problem that we are facing is what to do in London and many other major cities. How can we cut the pollution caused by motor vehicles? London should be the greatest park-and-ride system in the world, and many cities around the world could pattern themselves after us.

In the 1980s and 90s; the Government had a plan to build a park-and-ride system on the M1 motorway in London. The park-and-ride system would be multi-storey car park before JCT 4, at the old Elstree bus garage. The drivers would then take the public transport into London. Unfortunately, the Government shelved that plan and built a small business centre instead. What a mistake! That was a brilliant idea, which was not put into operation. At the end of all motorways, there should be a park-and-ride for public transport into London. That would cut pollution with one stroke and free up our congested roads.

CHAPTER 2

The Increase of the Motor Vehicle

As we can see daily, there are thousands of motor vehicles coming into London. The roads are congested and causing so much pollution. We need to look at the possibility of removing large numbers of vehicles from the roads.

If there were a park-and-ride system, one double-decker bus could take nearly 100 people to the capital. These commuters would not need to be caught in the congestion of traffic, feeling frustrated and raging. The drivers could then be more relaxed, reading the newspapers, and having a rest. Then in the evening, when they return from their work, they could pick up their vehicles and be on the motorways in minutes.

These park and rides could have hotels, restaurants, and all types of small businesses nearby. Just imagine how many jobs could be generated for hundreds of bus drivers and support staff.

Let us look at the possibility of a park-and-ride system on the M1 motorway, in London between JCT 3 and 4. It would also cater to drivers coming from the North on match days to the Wembley Stadium.

There is enough space near the end of all our motorways to build these multi-storey car parks, but is there the willpower to do something drastic to cut pollution? We say that we don't have insight, but this is just common sense—that we should plan for the future and put our plan into operation.

Rev. Michael Walker

I remember when the new government took over after the election of 1997; there were plans to build some more bypass and new roads. When the new government came into power, they decided to cancel all those plans, and no alternative plans were made.

If we do not plan for the future, we will fail, as we have seen today. We are now suffering because we did not plan; then we go into the future with no hope. It will cost us ten times more in the future than it would have cost in the past.

Let us build bridges, flyovers, underpasses, bypasses, and wider roads, where it is possible. Remember, we are in the twenty-first century,

And we need to progress, not stand still.

Where are the wise men and women of today? Let us rise up and defend our environment. People are dying while we are sleeping, and not talking about how to repair the damage that has been done. We need to call on our legislators, both National and Local, to give account for their lack of proper road planning, which is causing untold damage to the environment and to the health of the people.

When the Government is planning our roads, there should be information and consultation, providing a detailed look into the effects that these long-term plans will have on our environment.

Another benefit that we could get from having multi-storey car parks outside the city is that many car parks *in* the city could be turned into houses to help solve the housing crisis.

CHAPTER 3

Cyclists on the Road

It is appalling that so many cyclists are killed on the roads. Is there anything we can do to protect them?

We have allowed them to ride on busy roads without any training on how to be safe. In the old days, we had to train even pedestrians on how to cross the roads. We used the Green Cross Code to educate them to look right, then left, and right again; then if it was safe, you can cross. But today anyone can buy a bicycle and ride on the road without training. They don't obey red lights and put themselves in danger, along with others on the road. They ride on the sidewalks and put pedestrians in danger.

Now we have a cyclist who has killed a pedestrian, and he says that he did not know he shouldn't ride a cycle without adequate brakes so that he could stop without killing people. This is a shame on our government. Who have we elected to make laws to protect us; that didn't consider it necessary to make laws for cyclists?

Without laws, anarchy will prevail, and we have seen what is happening on the roads. Many lives are being lost because of our inaction.

I have seen cyclists go through red lights, and cars have had to stop quickly to avoid knocking them down. How long will we allow this blatant disregard for any laws?

Everyone that uses the roads should obey the law for their own safety, and that of others too.

Cyclists should be taught that they don't have a monopoly on the roads, and they should also ride with due care and attention, just as drivers must. Cyclists should be trained on how to ride safely, especially in areas where there is a lot of traffic. Also, the bicycle, should be fitted with a light and either bell or horn to warn others that they are there. This advice is vital.

When vehicles are turning into the path of the cyclist, the cyclist can see this traffic from the vehicle's turning signal. However, the cyclist does not know that the driver does not see him. The cyclist should pull back, for his own safety, and allow the vehicle to pass, or sound the horn or bell to warn the driver that he is there.

Cyclists should also be taught that there is a blind spot on vehicles, where the driver cannot see; in fact, they should always presume that the driver does *not* see them and pull back to let the driver turn. This is just a little courtesy that can save their lives.

Remember, the cyclist has no blind spots because there are no restrictions to their view. Why not think about safety and be courteous to others on the road?

Your life is precious, and your loved ones are waiting for your return home. They would be devastated upon hearing of your death.

Once again, please ride with due care and attention, and think about others. You are not alone on the road, so be cautious. Take these words of advice with you.

Cyclists need good roads to ride on, and in these days of cutbacks, they should contribute something for the upkeep-about fifty pounds a year, which should go solely to the fixing of the roads.

CHAPTER 4

The Pressure on the NHS and Our Hospitals

Because of current pollution in our environment, hospitals are stretched to the limit in trying to cope with the situation. What can be done to ease the pressure on our hospitals?

There are many measures that we can do to clean up our mess: making traffic flow more freely, driving more safely, (less arrogance and more courtesy). Drivers need to realise that when they cause an accident, they are putting more strain on the hospitals.

At this point, let me explain a little about the National Health Service (NHS). It was started in 1948 so that the poor people could have health care, and since then, it is free for all. Because of that, politicians play politics with it. They are afraid that if they do what needs to be done, they might lose votes at election time. They need to understand, that the population has increased dramatically since 1948, and we need to do what is necessary to help the poor people, not the rich ones.

It cannot be free for all today. There has to be a cut-off point, when some have to pay. Those who are getting very good wages should not expect to receive free health care.

Now, you may say, that they have to pay National Insurance. That should be preferably for free operations, if they need them. People who are earning good wages should not expect to get the little bit that the poor are getting.

Rev. Michael Walker

This change could help to plug the black hole, which is taking so much money.

You may say that we can't touch the funding for the NHS, but let me ask one question. If the men of old did not get it completely right, should we not try to make it right? Every year, we talk about how much money we have to put into it. Can we continue to pour money into it, knowing it is not enough? We need to take a long, hard look and come up with the right answers.

The next idea is, that when anyone goes to hospital, they should only receive bed and breakfast, and a light supper, with the exception of those who are on a special diet. You may ask me, then where will they get dinner from? There should be restaurants, and even fast foods shops, in our hospitals. Look at how many people go to visit the sick; they should be able to buy a dinner there, and all profits could go to the funding of hospital.

When I hear how many vacancies there are in the hospitals, I realize that we need to get back to the old ways here too.

In the old days, nurses were recruited, mainly from Africa, India, and the West Indies, and they were trained on the job. Many of those nurses became ward sisters, who were responsible for running the wards. They also recruited auxiliary nurses, who would help in the day-to-day work of the hospital to see that the wards were clean.

These nurses from the Commonwealth spoke English, but we have cast off the people from the Commonwealth and taken people from Europe and the Philippines instead, who cannot speak English. Let us go back to the Commonwealth and recruit people who can do the work, no matter what colour they are. Let us get rid of the institutional racism in our country and free up our people from the Commonwealth to do the work of building the mother country.

CHAPTER 5

Terrorism on the Roads

There is another hazard which we are facing on the roads, namely Terrorism, particularly the use of motor vehicles to kill or injure people. What can we do to stop this? Is there anything we can do?

I believe that we can stop them by protecting our pedestrians. We can put barriers (where there is room) alongside the sidewalks with steel and concrete or iron posts every few yards. In built-up areas, where many people have to walk together, there is a very easy way to put up spikes so that if a vehicle should jump the sidewalk, their tyres would be punctured.

We know the tactics of terrorists; let's counter them. Let's not sit back and wait until they break through and kill our people. We need to be one step ahead of them.

There is more that we can do. For example, on Hillside Road, London NW10, there are black iron pieces that resemble round pots, which the Council, have put on the sidewalks to prevent vehicles from parking. Those things would puncture and damage any vehicle.

In some areas, the sidewalks are too wide while the roads are too narrow. If there is an accident, then the road is blocked completely. There should always be two lanes on major roads, even if the road is one way. Pedestrians do not need to have so much room sidewalk to walk on. Here again steel posts should be put on the sidewalks to prevent vehicles from ploughing into pedestrians. A good example is those which the BBC Headquarters has put on the sidewalks at the Television Centre, London.

Our aim should be to puncture the tyres of vehicles that mount the pavement before they do any damage and kill pedestrians. We may complain about the cost, but should we put a price on protecting the lives of our people?

The police service, MI5, GCHQ, are doing a wonderful job of trying to keep us safe. We should give them the necessary tools to do the work in such a perilous, troubled, and dangerous world.

What do I mean by that? We have given them what is essentially a stick to subdue offenders if they resist arrest, but, given the times we are living in, with terrorists whose aim is to kill as many people as they can, I believe it is time that all police officers have Tasers for their personal protection.

I also think that they should be permitted to use them if they are in any danger of their lives, and they should be instructed that they must use it at the first sign of danger. If they make a mistake, then we should accept it as human error.

It is a disgrace to see our officers being slaughtered on duty, trying to keep us safe. The truncheon has not protected them; it is out-dated and must be replaced by a more effective means of self-defence. If anyone attacks you, you should have the right to defend yourself. Our officers should have that in place right now. They are not there on their own agenda; we have given them a work to do. Let us give them the proper tools to do the job.

Let us try to keep the people safe on the roads, even if it means paying a little more in taxes for this purpose. I don't think that anyone would complain about helping to pay for the safety of our pedestrians and our police officers.

Pollution

At this time, the UK government has been taken to court for not dealing with pollution, and they are asking for more time. However, the court did not give them any more time because we need to do it now.

There should also be a furnace to burn the majority of waste, God created fire to consume and destroy things.

Now here is the answer from a man of God. Will the nations of the world take it and put it into operation so that we can breathe cleaner air and be safe, as we go about our daily business? Maybe they won't, because it seems that the National and Civic leaders have cast off the Spiritual leaders.

They think that they do not need us to tell them what to do. This is a short-sighted view that will lead us into chaos and calamity; Spiritual leaders are a vital part of our community, and they should be treated as such. They should be encouraged to take part in the temporal and the spiritual lives of the people.

I heard a radio programme from China a few years ago which said their leaders have a time, every three months, to consult the community in order to get ideas. But here in the Western world our leaders seem to think that once they are elected by the people, they don't need to take advice from the community. Whatever you may say to them it has no effect because they think that they always know best.

The councils can do whatsoever they want. We are paying them their wages, and we have to accept what they do, even if it destroys our community. No one can oppose them; we are helpless to do anything. Is this what we call democracy? May the God of heaven help us?

CONCLUSION

The whole Earth is suffering from the effects of the neglect of our environment. Something needs to be done, and done now—not tomorrow, but today. If we continue to neglect the problem, we do so at our own peril. What should we do now? We should begin a deep clean-up of the earth. We should begin to disinfect our streets, our shopping centres and where a lot of people have to walk. When we do this we will begin to kill the bugs which will infect us, and eventually kill us.

When we look at the North Pole, the ice is melting at an alarming rate. When that happens, the seas will rise and many islands will face flooding.

Let us do what we can now to clean up our cities so that our people can breathe cleaner air. Those who suffer from asthma will breathe more easily, and that will free up the hospitals to deal with other cases. The NHS is at the breaking point; whatever we can do to help, we should do now so that the hospitals can continue to do the wonderful work they are doing.

Let us plan our cities better and widen the roads so that they can cope with the traffic. It is an injustice to the community when planners put all the traffic on the major roads and block off the side roads, which were designed to ease traffic. Then they complain about the bottlenecks that their actions are causing. Motor vehicles are not our enemy; they are one of the best means of travel. The problem is that short-sighted planning is keeping vehicles on the roads longer than necessary. It would be good if the planners could acknowledge their mistakes and put things right instead of believing that they are right all the time.

I was a private hire driver for thirty-one years, working on the roads daily. I have seen the silly planning of the roads.

I have also noticed that roads which could help reduce the congestion are often closed. In some areas, two roads in a row are one-ways *in the same direction.* Cars can enter the major road but cannot exit it. To me that is daft planning. In my forty-eight years of driving, I have loved to drive on the side roads and avoid traffic, but now some of these side roads are closed. I can understand if they do not want larger vehicles on them, but then the solution is to bring back width limits so that only small cars can pass through.

Let us get some people in the national government and the local councils who will know what to do so that we can free up our roads. Why should we sit back and watch our communities being destroyed because of people who are without vision and knowledge?

Now that we have come to the end of this book, may the good Lord of heaven help us to return to the good old ways so that he can bless us and guide us again. We have gone astray, following our own devices, and we are reaping the rewards of our actions. If we begin to change, he will surely heal our lands.

ABOUT THE AUTHOR

Rev. Walker is an ordained Minister of Religion for over forty years. He is the founder and Senior Pastor of the Church of God Revival Ministries in Willesden London.

He was born the fifth child of a family of thirteen children.

He is a father of six children, six grandchildren, and four great grandchildren.

He has counselled many families when they were going through various problems. He has seen the good results from those counselling.

He also conducts a daily Gospel Radio programme on www.hot96.co.uk from 7-10 am. This Radio Ministry is a blessing to many nations of the world. From the many positive feedbacks of consistent listeners it has prompted him to pen this pertinent edition.

ABOUT THE BOOK

This book can be very helpful to those who find it hard to talk to people about their problems.

Those who find it hard to interact with other people, whose lives are so hectic, with work and children, which are so demanding, they can't even find time to go to Church. He wants them to have the consolation that God is right by their side and they are not alone. We also have the assurance that he is always willing to help them when they call out to him.

Looking at the situation of the world in which we are living in today and observing the suffering and pain that the nations are going through; I have always sought to find a solution whenever any problems arise in life.

When I study the Bible the (Word of God) I find that he has given us the solutions, but it seems that we refuse to accept his guidance and seek to find our own answers,but sad to say that our answers do not help us.

When God Created the World he put everything in motion to sustain life.

And to heal our Sickness and Diseases. We have however; gone so far away from his teachings and we have now developed our own ways and rejected his way, and because of that we are reaping the reward of our doing.

Rev. Michael Walker

My advice is that we seek to find his will and his way and try to obey it.

Let us not forget the words of Jesus Christ who told us that God is our Father and as Father he has the responsibility for our well-being.

Thank you for buying this book may the God of Heaven bless you.

Signed with love from
Rev. M. Walker

www.ingramcontent.com/pod-product-compliance
Lightning Source LLC
Chambersburg PA
CBHW052111110526
44592CB00013B/1572